My United States
Michigan

JOSH GREGORY

Children's Press®
An Imprint of Scholastic Inc.

Content Consultant
James Wolfinger, PhD, Associate Dean and Professor
College of Education, DePaul University, Chicago, Illinois

Library of Congress Cataloging-in-Publication Data
Names: Gregory, Josh, author.
Title: Michigan / by Josh Gregory.
Description: New York, NY : Children's Press, 2017. | Series: A true book | Includes bibliographical references and index.
Identifiers: LCCN 2017002483 | ISBN 9780531252604 (library binding) | ISBN 9780531232903 (pbk.)
Subjects: LCSH: Michigan—Juvenile literature.
Classification: LCC F566.3 .G68 2017 | DDC 977.4—dc23
LC record available at https://lccn.loc.gov/2017002483

Photographs ©: cover: Dan Sheehan/Getty Images; back cover ribbon: AliceLiddelle/Getty Images; back cover bottom: Jim West/The Image Works; 3 map: Jim McMahon; 3 bottom: Joseph Sohm/Shutterstock; 4 right: LiliGraphie/Shutterstock; 4 left: Gerald A. DeBoer/Shutterstock; 5 bottom: Gary Kramer/U.S. Fish & Wildlife Service; 5 top: Suzanne Tucker/Shutterstock; 6 inset: Wildnerdpix/Shutterstock; 7 top: Travel_Bug/Thinkstock; 7 bottom: falun/Thinkstock; 7 center: Stan Rohrer/Alamy Images; 8-9: James Brey/iStockphoto; 11: John A Gessner Photography/Getty Images; 12: Jamie A. MacDonald/Getty Images; 13: Terrance Klassen/age fotostock; 14: Gary Kramer/U.S. Fish & Wildlife Service; 15: Manuel Romaris/Getty Images; 16-17: Henryk Sadura/Shutterstock; 19: Sacco/ZUMAPRESS.com/Alamy Images; 20: Tigatelu/Dreamstime; 22 right: PhotoRoman/Shutterstock; 22 left: Atlaspix/Shutterstock; 23 top left: LiliGraphie/Shutterstock; 23 bottom: FotoRequest/Shutterstock; 23 center left: simplycmb/Thinkstock; 23 top right: Gerald A. DeBoer/Shutterstock; 23 center: Science History Images/Alamy Images; 23 center right: imageBROKER/Superstock, Inc.; 24-25: William Albert Allard/Getty Images; 27: Underwood Archives/The Image Works; 29: Superstock, Inc.; 30 center: North Wind Picture Archives/AP Images; 30 left: Stan Rohrer/Alamy Images; 30 right: Superstock, Inc.; 31 bottom left: Everett Collection Inc./age fotostock; 31 top left: Atlaspix/Shutterstock; 31 bottom right: Bill Pugliano/Getty Images; 31 top right: falun/Thinkstock; 32: Bill Pugliano/Getty Images; 33: Historical/Getty Images; 34-35: Tony Spina/MCT/Newscom; 35 inset: Steve Kagan/Getty Images; 36: Jim West/Alamy Images; 37: Clark Brennan/Alamy Images; 38: Historical/Getty Images; 39 main: Dennis Macdonald/Getty Images; 39 inset: imageBROKER/Jim West/Newscom; 40 bottom: margouillat photo/Shutterstock; 40 background: PepitoPhotos/iStockphoto; 41: Suzanne Tucker/Shutterstock; 42 top left: Library of Congress; 42 top right: Marvin Lichtner/Getty Images; 42 bottom left: Sbukley/Dreamstime; 42 bottom right: AP Images; 43 top left: Imagecollect/Dreamstime; 43 top right: Everett Collection Inc./age fotostock; 43 center: ARNOLDO MONDADORI EDITORE S.P./age fotostock; 43 bottom left: Jerry Coli/Dreamstime; 43 bottom center: Jeff Chiu/AP Images; 43 bottom right: Juergen Hasenkopf/imageBROKER/age fotostock; 44 bottom: Michael Szönyi/imageBROKER/age fotostock; 44 top: davidf/iStockphoto; 44 center: Suzanne Tucker/Shutterstock; 45 center: Space Chimp/Shutterstock; 45 top: Sean Proctor/The New York Times/Redux; 45 bottom: John A Gessner Photography/Getty Images.

Maps by Map Hero, Inc.

SCHOLASTIC, CHILDREN'S PRESS, A TRUE BOOK™, and associated logos are trademarks and/or registered trademarks of Scholastic Inc., 557 Broadway, New York, NY 10012.
1 2 3 4 5 6 7 8 9 10 R 27 26 25 24 23 22 21 20 19 18

Front cover: A wave crashing against the lighthouse at Grand Haven

Back cover: A car on the assembly line at the Detroit-Hamtramck assembly plant

Welcome to Michigan

Find the Truth!

Everything you are about to read is true *except* for one of the sentences on this page.

Which one is **TRUE**?

T or F Michigan is divided into two unconnected areas of land.

T or F Michigan was one of the 13 original U.S. states.

UNITED STATES

Michigan

MICHIGAN
BJZ097
76

Find the answers in this book.

3

Contents

Apple blossoms

THE BIG TRUTH!

What Represents Michigan?

Painted
turtle

A family on a boat trip

Gray wolf

This Is Michigan!

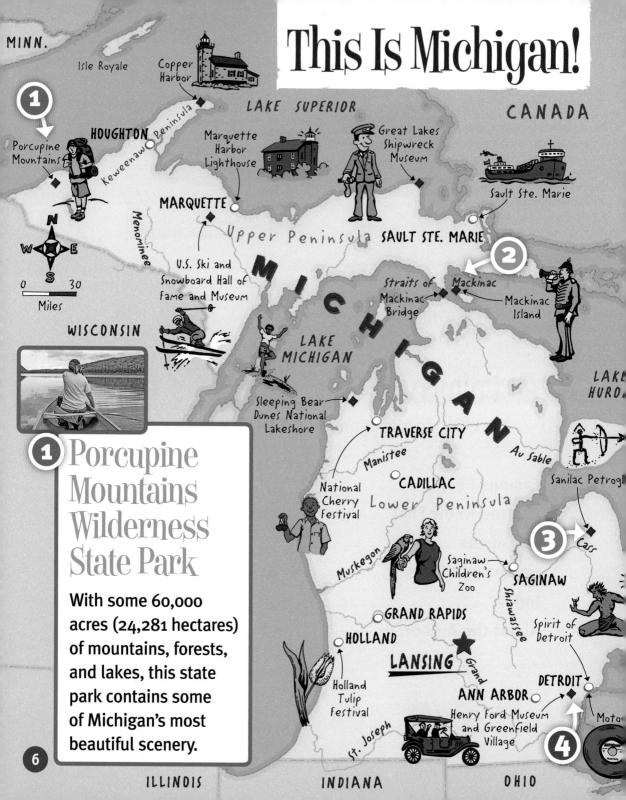

MINN.

Isle Royale

Copper Harbor

LAKE SUPERIOR

CANADA

1 Porcupine Mountains

HOUGHTON

Keweenaw Peninsula

Marquette Harbor Lighthouse

Great Lakes Shipwreck Museum

Sault Ste. Marie

N W E S

0 30 Miles

MARQUETTE

Menominee

Upper Peninsula

MICHIGAN

SAULT STE. MARIE

2

Straits of Mackinac Bridge

Mackinac

Mackinac Island

WISCONSIN

U.S. Ski and Snowboard Hall of Fame and Museum

LAKE MICHIGAN

LAKE HURON

Sleeping Bear Dunes National Lakeshore

TRAVERSE CITY

Manistee

Au Sable

Sanilac Petroglyph

National Cherry Festival

CADILLAC

Lower Peninsula

1 Porcupine Mountains Wilderness State Park

With some 60,000 acres (24,281 hectares) of mountains, forests, and lakes, this state park contains some of Michigan's most beautiful scenery.

Muskegon

Saginaw Children's Zoo

3 Cass

SAGINAW

Shiawassee

Spirit of Detroit

GRAND RAPIDS

HOLLAND

LANSING

Grand

DETROIT

Holland Tulip Festival

ANN ARBOR

Henry Ford Museum and Greenfield Village

Moto

4

St. Joseph

6

ILLINOIS

INDIANA

OHIO

② Mackinac Island

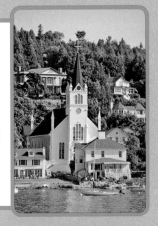

This island is located in Lake Huron between the Upper and Lower **Peninsulas**. With its beautiful landscapes and preserved historic buildings, it is one of Michigan's most popular tourist attractions.

③ Sanilac Petroglyphs

These petroglyphs, or rock carvings, were created by Native Americans hundreds of years ago. They are the only known Native American rock carvings in the state.

NEW YORK

CANADA

LAKE ONTARIO

④ The Henry Ford Museum

Named for the founder of the Ford Motor Company, this museum in Dearborn contains historic automobiles and a number of important artifacts from U.S. history.

LAKE ERIE

PENNYSLVANIA

The name Michigan comes from a Native American word for "great lake."

CHAPTER 1

Land and Wildlife

Located at the northern end of the midwestern United States, Michigan is a land of tremendous natural beauty. There are several major rivers, thousands of lakes, and many scenic waterfalls. Michigan has rugged mountains, forested hills, and sandy dunes. The state's diverse landscape provides a rich environment for a wide variety of plants and animals.

Two Sides to the State

Michigan is divided into two main pieces of land. To the north is the long, narrow Upper Peninsula. To the south, across Lake Michigan and Lake Huron, lies the mitten-shaped Lower Peninsula. The two peninsulas are connected by the Mackinac Bridge, which spans a narrow passageway of water called the Straits of Mackinac that links Lake Michigan and Lake Huron.

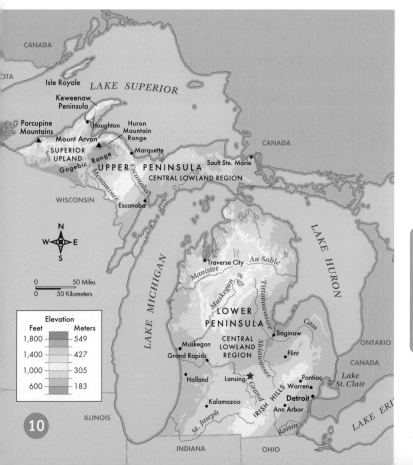

This map shows where the higher (yellow and orange) and lower (dark green) areas of the state are.

The Great Lakes

The Great Lakes are a collection of five huge North American lakes: Lake Michigan, Lake Huron, Lake Superior, Lake Erie, and Lake Ontario. Combined, they make up the largest body of freshwater in the world. Michigan is connected to four of these lakes. For this reason, Michigan is often called the Great Lakes State. Only Lake Ontario does not touch the state's border.

Changing Seasons

Michigan gets a taste of all kinds of weather as the seasons change each year. In summer, you can look forward to high temperatures and plenty of sunshine. In fall, the weather turns pleasantly cool, and the leaves on the trees change color. Winter brings cold temperatures and plenty of snow and ice. By the time spring rolls around, you'll be ready for some breezy, warm weather.

MAXIMUM
TEMPERATURE
112°F

MINIMUM
TEMPERATURE
-51°F

Cows huddle close together to stay warm during a Michigan snowstorm.

Michigan is home to four national forests.

Trees Everywhere

Long ago, almost all of the land that now makes up Michigan was covered in thick forests. As more humans began living there, they cut down many of the area's trees. But even today, about 40 percent of Michigan is covered in forestland, making it one of the most heavily forested states. You'll find all kinds of trees growing there, from spruce and pine to oak, hickory, and maple.

Forest Life

Michigan's forests are home to a range of animal **species,** from bears and deer to rabbits and raccoons. Eagles and geese fly above as turkeys waddle along the ground. One forest animal nearly disappeared, however: the gray wolf. Humans hunted this predator in the 1900s. By 1973, six wolves remained in the Upper Peninsula, plus another small population on Isle Royale in Lake Superior. But thanks to government protection, the state's wolf population is now up to about 600.

Gray wolves have made an impressive comeback in Michigan.

Aquatic Animals

With its lakes, rivers, and streams, Michigan is home to plenty of aquatic life. Beavers build dams, and frogs and toads hop along the shorelines. Waterways teem with bass, catfish, trout, perch, and other fish. Canadian geese stop by on their way south in the winter and north in the summer. Game birds include pheasant, partridge, ducks, and wild geese.

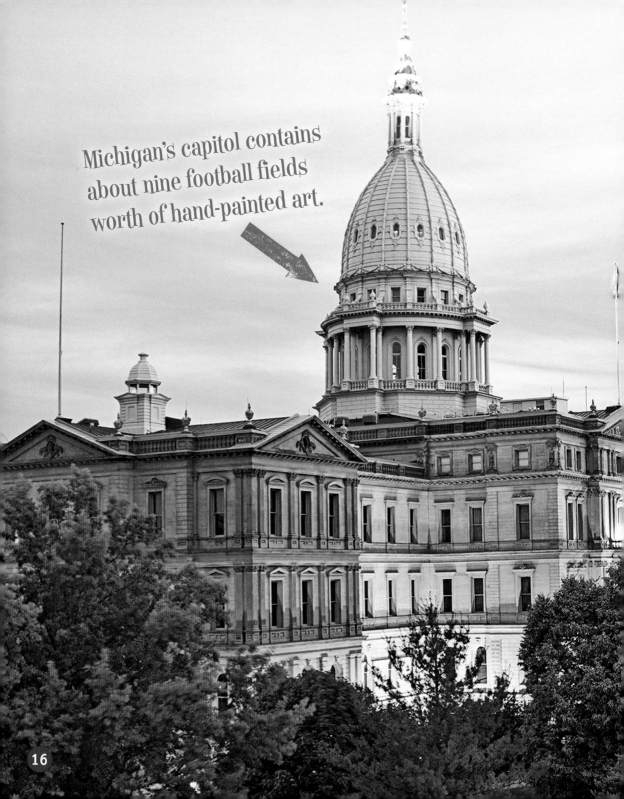

Michigan's capitol contains about nine football fields worth of hand-painted art.

CHAPTER 2

Government

When Michigan became a state in 1837, its capital was Detroit, its largest city. However, Detroit is located far in the southeastern corner of the state. It was difficult to travel there from certain areas, such as the Upper Peninsula. As a result, the capital was moved to the more central location of Lansing in 1847. Today, this is where Michigan's many government officials meet to make, carry out, and **interpret** the state's laws.

State Government Basics

Michigan's state government has three branches. The governor leads the executive branch, which oversees the budget, as well as law enforcement, education, and other systems.

The lawmaking legislative branch has two houses: a Senate and a House of Representatives.

The judges and courts of the judicial branch hear the cases of people accused of breaking the law.

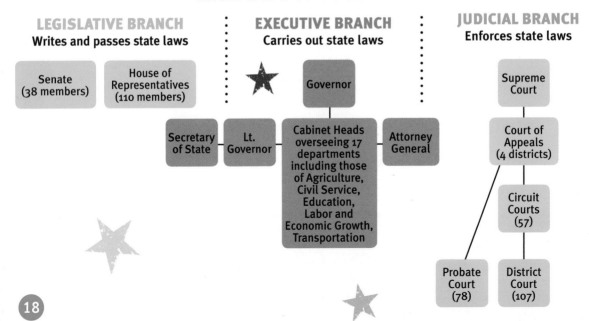

MICHIGAN'S STATE GOVERNMENT

LEGISLATIVE BRANCH
Writes and passes state laws

EXECUTIVE BRANCH
Carries out state laws

JUDICIAL BRANCH
Enforces state laws

Senate
(38 members)

House of Representatives
(110 members)

Governor

Supreme Court

Secretary of State

Lt. Governor

Cabinet Heads overseeing 17 departments including those of Agriculture, Civil Service, Education, Labor and Economic Growth, Transportation

Attorney General

Court of Appeals
(4 districts)

Circuit Courts
(57)

Probate Court
(78)

District Court
(107)

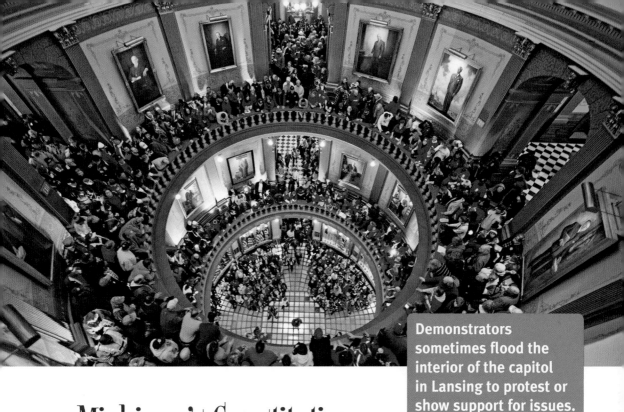

Michigan's Constitution

The details of Michigan's government and legal system are laid out in the state's constitution. This document was originally created in 1835 and was revised in 1850. Since then, Michigan lawmakers have made several additions, or amendments, to the constitution. Amendments allow the state government to adapt as times change and situations arise that were not mentioned in the original constitution.

Michigan in the National Government

Each state sends elected officials to represent it in the U.S. Congress. Like every state, Michigan has two senators. The U.S. House of Representatives relies on a state's population to determine its numbers. Michigan has 14 representatives in the House.

Every four years, states vote on the next U.S. president. Each state is granted a number of electoral votes based on its number of members in Congress. With two senators and 14 representatives, Michigan has 16 electoral votes.

2 senators and 14 representatives

16 electoral votes

With 16 electoral votes, Michigan's voice in president elections is above average compared to other states.

Representing Michigan

Elected officials in Michigan represent a population
with a range of interests, lifestyles, and backgrounds.

Ethnicity (2015 estimates)

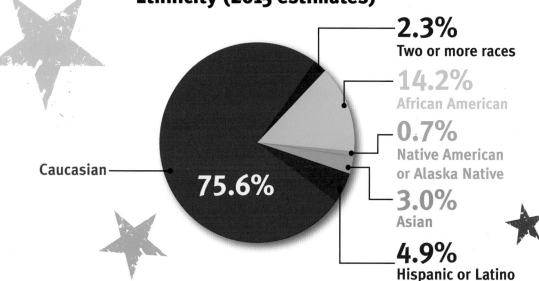

2.3%
Two or more races

14.2%
African American

0.7%
Native American
or Alaska Native

3.0%
Asian

4.9%
Hispanic or Latino

Caucasian

75.6%

27%
of the population
have a degree
beyond high
school.

71% own their
own homes.

72% live in
cities.

90%
of the
population
graduated from
high school.

6% of Michigan residents were
born in other countries.

9% speak a language other
than English at home.

What Represents Michigan?

States choose specific animals, plants, and objects to represent the values and characteristics of the land and its people. Find out why these symbols were chosen to represent Michigan or discover surprising curiosities about them.

Seal

Michigan's seal depicts some of the state's native animals around a shield reading *tuebor*, which means "I will defend" in Latin. The man on the shield is raising his right hand in a gesture of peace, but he also holds a rifle in his left hand, meaning that he is ready to defend his state.

Flag

Michigan has had three different flags since it became a state. The current one was adopted in 1911. It consists of a blue field with the state seal displayed in the center.

Apple Blossom

STATE FLOWER

Michigan's native apple blossoms are known for their fragrance and beauty.

Painted Turtle

STATE REPTILE

A group of fifth graders chose this little turtle as the state reptile in 1995.

Mastodon

STATE FOSSIL

People have found mastodon fossils in more than 250 places across Michigan.

Petoskey Stone

STATE STONE

These stones are the fossils of corals that lived in Michigan 350 million years ago.

Dwarf Lake Iris

STATE WILDFLOWER

This flower grows only along Lakes Michigan and Huron.

American Robin

STATE BIRD

Nearly 200,000 people voted in 1931 on what the state bird should be. The American robin won.

Ojibwe people traditionally lived across a large area, including what are now Michigan, Minnesota, and southern Canada.

CHAPTER 3

History

The United States was formed in 1776, and Michigan didn't become a state until 1837. However, people lived in the area for thousands of years before that. Humans first reached the area sometime around 11,000 BCE. They hunted animals such as caribou using homemade spears of wood and stone. Over time, they became more advanced. They invented new tools, formed settlements, and developed unique cultures.

A Land of Many Cultures

Many different cultures developed in Michigan as early people settled there. Each had its own language, traditions, and way of life. The Hopewell people are famous for building huge burial mounds. Some of these incredible structures still stand today. The Ojibwas, Odawas, and Potawatomis formed an alliance called the Council of Three Fires. They traded goods, which helped all three groups flourish. Other Native Americans living in Michigan included Hurons, Menominees, Foxes, Sauks, and Miamis.

This map shows the general areas where Native American groups settled.

Ojibwe people made canoes using birchbark.

Native American Life

Many of Michigan's Native American people lived in homes called wigwams. These structures were shaped like domes. People built them using wood and animal skins. Near their homes, native people farmed a variety of crops, including beans, corn, squash, and melons. They also hunted in the area's forests and took to the lakes in handmade canoes to catch fish.

Explorers From Abroad

The first Europeans in the land now known as Michigan were French explorers, who arrived in the 1600s. Searching for a sailing route to China, they instead found themselves in the Great Lakes. The many natural resources they found encouraged them to stay. Fur trappers came to the area in search of beaver, fox, and other animals. Their furs were in high demand in Europe. French **missionaries** also came, hoping to convert Native Americans to their religion.

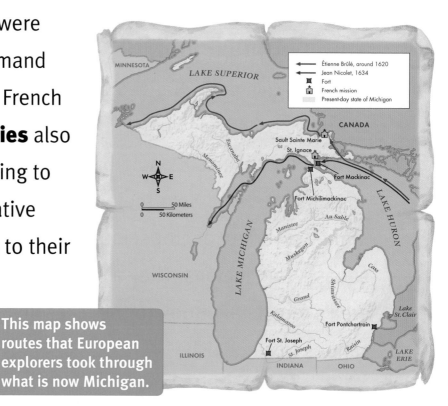

This map shows routes that European explorers took through what is now Michigan.

The French and Indian War helped establish Great Britain's control over what became the 13 colonies.

The French and Indian War

Overall, Native Americans and the new French settlers got along well. In 1754, they joined forces to fight Great Britain's American **colonists** in the French and Indian War. During the war, the French were driven out, leaving Michigan's Native Americans alone in the fight against the British. By 1763, the war was over, and more British people began flooding into the area. This forced many Native Americans to leave their homes and head westward.

Becoming a State

Between 1775 and 1783, the British settlers in North America battled Great Britain for their independence. This led to the creation of the United States. At first, the newly formed country consisted of only 13 states along the East Coast. However, it gradually expanded to the west, and new states were created. In 1837, Michigan became the 26th state.

Timeline of Michigan Events

11,000 BCE
People first come to Michigan.

1754–1763
The people of Michigan fight in the French and Indian War.

11,000 BCE → 1600s CE → 1754–1763

1600s CE
Europeans begin to explore and settle in the area.

A Growing Population

The 19th century was a time of rapid growth in Michigan. Thanks to the creation of New York's Erie Canal in 1825, boats could travel easily from the Atlantic Ocean to the Great Lakes. This made it much easier for people to reach Michigan from the coast. Hundreds of thousands of people traveled to the state to start farms and build homes and towns. Unfortunately, this forced even more Native Americans out of the area.

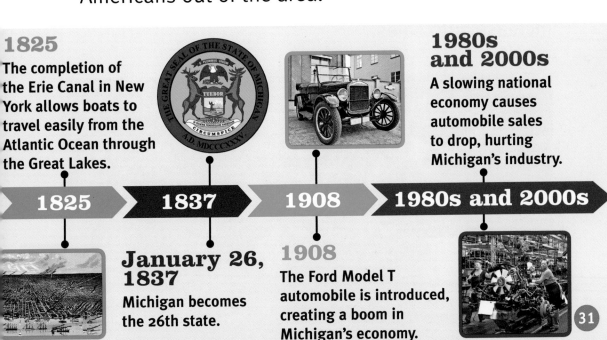

1825
The completion of the Erie Canal in New York allows boats to travel easily from the Atlantic Ocean through the Great Lakes.

1980s and 2000s
A slowing national economy causes automobile sales to drop, hurting Michigan's industry.

1825 **1837** **1908** **1980s and 2000s**

January 26, 1837
Michigan becomes the 26th state.

1908
The Ford Model T automobile is introduced, creating a boom in Michigan's economy.

Ups and Downs

During the 1800s, manufacturing grew in Michigan, providing jobs for many people. The auto industry took off in the 1900s and became the base of the state's economy. But **recessions** in the 1980s and 2000s, along with competition from overseas car companies, slowed the American auto industry. Many people lost their jobs. Things have been looking up in recent years, though. Electric cars, computerized cars, and other new types of vehicles have helped increase auto sales.

The GM assembly plant in Flint employs more than 3,000 people.

Henry Ford

Perhaps no one person brought more change to Michigan than automobile pioneer Henry Ford. The introduction of Ford's Model T car in 1908 marked the beginning of an era when automobiles became the most popular form of transportation. A lifelong Michigan resident, Ford established his company's headquarters near Detroit. Other motor companies, such as General Motors and Chrysler, also made the city their home. This brought a huge number of jobs to the state, and Michigan experienced an economic boom during the 20th century.

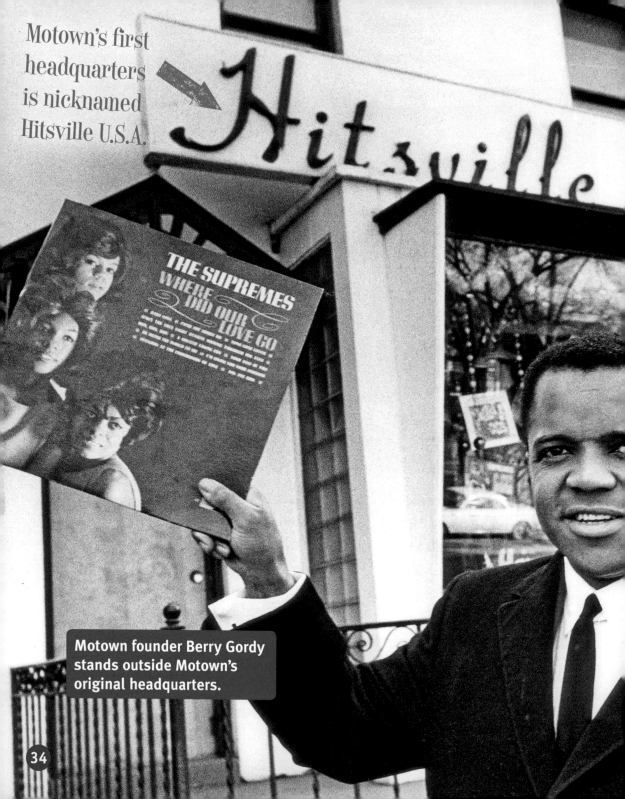

Motown's first headquarters is nicknamed Hitsville U.S.A.

Motown founder Berry Gordy stands outside Motown's original headquarters.

CHAPTER 4

Culture

From the streets of Detroit to the secluded **rural** areas of the Upper Peninsula, Michigan is home to a wide range of lifestyles. There are museums, theaters, galleries, and more across the state. Michigan is especially famous for its music scene, including the legendary Motown record company. Motown has released music from artists such as Stevie Wonder, Marvin Gaye, the Supremes, and Michael Jackson.

Berry Gordy and several Motown artists sing together at Motown studios.

Sports and Recreation

Most of Michigan's pro sports teams have their home base in Detroit. The state's football fans root for the Lions, while basketball fans cheer on the Pistons. Hockey is especially popular in Michigan. The Detroit Red Wings have won the Stanley Cup championship 11 times since the team was founded in 1926. And the Detroit Tigers have been playing professional baseball since 1894! In addition to pro teams, Michiganians also love watching the state's many college sports teams compete.

Many Michiganians of all ages play hockey.

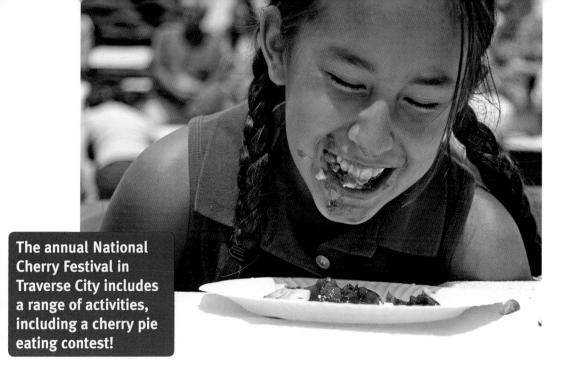

The annual National Cherry Festival in Traverse City includes a range of activities, including a cherry pie eating contest!

Celebrating in Michigan

Michigan is home to many local celebrations and traditions. In June, head to Battle Creek for a taste of the state's famous breakfast cereals at CerealFest. Different parts of the state host cherry festivals, strawberry festivals, maple syrup festivals, and other events celebrating Michigan's local specialties. If you like art, go to Ann Arbor in July to check out the annual art fairs downtown.

In earlier times, many Michiganians found jobs in logging. It was, however, physically demanding work with low pay and long hours.

Off to Work

While the auto industry has declined from its peak in the 20th century, it is still a major force in Michigan. Agriculture is another big moneymaker. Farmers grow fruits, vegetables, beans, and many other crops. With so many forests, timber is also an important resource. Thousands of workers grow and cut down trees. Michigan is also a center of the breakfast cereal industry. Two well-known cereal companies, Kellogg's and Post, are based in the state.

Changing Technology, Changing Jobs

One way Michigan is adapting to the modern economy is by using new types of energy. For example, electric cars are becoming more and more important to the auto industry. Also, the state has built many wind farms. On a wind farm, **turbines** generate electricity as the blowing wind turns their blades. This allows the people of Michigan to use electricity without burning **fossil fuels**. This alternative energy source is much better for the environment.

Electric car

Meals in Michigan

The people of Michigan love to enjoy their state's fresh, locally grown fruits. Apples and cherries are especially popular. They are eaten raw or turned into baked treats, cider, and more. Locally caught fish is another delicacy. People order it at restaurants, buy it at markets, and catch it themselves. Polish, German, and Middle Eastern cuisines are also very popular in many parts of the state.

★ **Baked Apples** ★

Ask an adult to help you!

Ingredients
4 Michigan apples
1/2 cup brown sugar
4 tablespoons butter
2 teaspoons cinnamon

Directions
Cut out most of each apple's core, leaving some at the bottom to hold the other ingredients. In a bowl, combine the brown sugar, butter, and cinnamon. Stuff the hole in each apple with one-quarter of this mix. Bake the apples in a 375 degree oven for about 30 minutes, and enjoy!

Explore Michigan!

There are plenty of incredible sights and things to do throughout Michigan. Enjoy a boat ride on the Great Lakes, hike through a forest in the Upper Peninsula, or visit the state's many museums. Whether you're a lifelong Michiganian or a first time visitor, you're sure to have a good time! ★

Boat trips on Michigan's many lakes are a popular activity for families.

Famous People

Sojourner Truth

(1797–1883) was an activist who was born into slavery and later fought against it after escaping to freedom. She lived in Battle Creek for many years.

Malcolm X

(1925–1965) was a religious leader and activist who fought for the rights of African Americans. He grew up in Lansing.

Berry Gordy

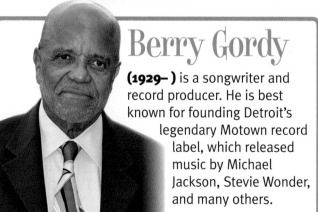

(1929–) is a songwriter and record producer. He is best known for founding Detroit's legendary Motown record label, which released music by Michael Jackson, Stevie Wonder, and many others.

Francis Ford Coppola

(1939–) is a filmmaker who is most famous for directing such movies as *The Godfather*, *Apocalypse Now*, and *The Conversation*. He was born in Detroit.

Lily Tomlin

(1939–) is an award-winning comedian and actress who has appeared in many films, TV series, and plays. She is from Detroit.

Aretha Franklin

(1942–) is a singer and songwriter who has won 18 Grammy Awards, sold 75 million albums, and scored dozens of hit singles. She grew up in Detroit.

Madonna

(1958–) is a singer and actress who is one of the most successful pop stars of all time. She is from Bay City.

Magic Johnson

(1959–) is a businessman and former professional basketball star who is considered one of the game's all-time greatest players. He is from Lansing.

Larry Page

(1973–) is a co-founder of Google, one of the world's biggest technology companies. He is from East Lansing.

Serena Williams

(1981–) is widely considered to be one of the greatest tennis players of all time. She was born in Saginaw.

Did You Know That ...

As home to a massive manufacturer of magic supplies, Colon is considered the Magic Capital of the World.

At 5 miles (8 kilometers), Mackinac Bridge is the longest **suspension bridge** in the Western Hemisphere. In very strong winds, the center section of the bridge moves!

Michigan has more freshwater shoreline than any other state.

The world's first floating zip code is located in Michigan. It is served by the *J. W. Westcott II*, a mail boat that delivers letters and packages to and from ships on the Detroit River.

A Detroit police officer invented the three-color, four-way traffic light. The first light of this kind was installed on Detroit's Woodward Avenue in 1920.

Did you find the truth?

T Michigan is divided into two unconnected areas of land.

F Michigan was one of the 13 original U.S. states.

Resources

Books

Nonfiction

Gregory, Josh. *Henry Ford: Father of the Auto Industry*. New York: Children's Press, 2014.

Raatma, Lucia. *Michigan*. New York: Children's Press, 2014.

Fiction

Curtis, Christopher Paul. *Bud, not Buddy*. New York: Delacorte Press, 1999.

Erdich, Louise. *The Birchbark House*. New York: Hyperion Books for Children, 1999.

Rinaldi, Ann. *Girl in Blue*. New York: Scholastic, 2001.

Movies

Dreamgirls (2006)

The Karate Kid (2010)

Mr. Mom (1983)

The Polar Express (2004)

Somewhere in Time (1980)

Visit this Scholastic website for more information on Michigan:
★ www.factsfornow.scholastic.com
Enter the keyword **Michigan**

Important Words

colonists (KAH-luh-nistz) people who live in a colony or who help establish one

fossil fuels (FAH-suhl FYOO-uhlz) coal, oil, or natural gas, formed from the remains of prehistoric plants and animals

interpret (in-TUR-prit) to figure out what something means

missionaries (MISH-uh-ner-eez) people who are sent to a foreign country to teach about religion and do good works

peninsulas (puh-NIN-suh-luhz) pieces of land that stick out from a larger landmass and are almost completely surrounded by water

recessions (ri-SESH-uhnz) times when business slows down and more workers than usual are unemployed

rural (ROOR-uhl) of or having to do with the countryside, country life, or farming

species (SPEE-sheez) one of the groups into which animals and plants are divided

suspension bridge (suh-SPEN-shuhn BRIJ) a bridge that hangs from cables

turbines (TUR-buhnz) engines powered by water, steam, wind, or gas passing through the blades of a wheel and making it spin

Index

Page numbers in **bold** indicate illustrations.

About the Author

Josh Gregory is the author of more than 100 books for kids. He has written about everything from animals to technology to history. A graduate of the University of Missouri–Columbia, he currently lives in Portland, Oregon.